Samuel French Acting Edition

Rule of Thumb

by Agatha Christie

SAMUELFRENCH.COM SAMUELFRENCH.CO.UK

ISBN 978-0-573-03104-5
concordtheatricals.co.uk
concordtheatricals.com
www.agathachristielimited.com

For Production Enquiries

United Kingdom and World Excluding North America
licensing@concordtheatricals.co.uk
020-7054-7200

United States and Canada
Info@concordtheatricals.com
1-866-979-0447

Each title is subject to availability from Samuel French, depending upon country of performance.

MUSIC USE NOTE

IMPORTANT BILLING AND CREDIT REQUIREMENTS

TABLE OF CONTENTS

The Rats

CHARACTERS

SANDRA GREY
JENNIFER BRICE
DAVID FORRESTER
ALEC HANBURY

THE RATS was first presented by Peter Saunders at the Duchess Theatre, London on 20 December 1962. The performance was directed by Hubert Gregg, with sets by Peter Rice. The cast was as follows:

SANDRA GREY .... Betty McDowall
JENNIFER BRICE .... Mercy Haystead
DAVID FORRESTER .... David Langton
ALEC HANBURY .... Raymond Bowers

(The Michael Torrance's flat in Hampstead. A fine summer evening, about 6:30 p.m. The flat is a studio. There is a door leading on to a small balcony and a long window running across the back showing a view over the roof tops. Inside there is the front door and a hallway leading to the bathroom and kitchenette. Below the window is a very big chest, known as a Damascus Bridal Chest, dark wood studded with ornamental brass nails. Prominent is a line of Baghdad coffee pots with large beaked spouts. There are also one or two pieces of Persian or Islamic pottery and a Kurdish knife held in a sheaf. Otherwise the furnishings of the flat are severely modern. There is a big double divan covered with cushions and a low table with modern armchairs either side of it. On the table is a tray with drinks and a few glasses. There is also a budgerigar in a cage. The entrance buzzer and knocker sound. This is repeated impatiently then **SANDRA***'s voice is heard offstage.)*

SANDRA. *(Offstage.)* Anyone there? Anyone at home?

(She knocks on the door and gives a surprised exclamation as it opens. **SANDRA** *enters. She is a smart and very attractive woman of thirty.)*

Pat – Michael?

(She looks around then crosses to the hallway, exits, re-enters, then moves to the balcony door and looks out. Puzzled, she removes her wrap, puts it over the back of an armchair

then sits. She reaches for a cigarette box on the coffee table but finds it empty. Taking one from her handbag she lights it then gets up and walks about, puffing with increasing irritability.)

How extraordinary!

(She glances at her watch.)

Nice manners, I must say.

(She goes out on to the balcony. There is the sound of a key in the lock.)

JENNIFER. *(Offstage.)* Oh, it's open!

*(***JENNIFER*** pushes the door and enters. She is a vacant faced young woman of thirty-odd, a bit of a cat and not so silly as she seems. She has rather an affected manner. Seeing the wrap, she stops and turns towards the balcony.)*

Hello, Sandra.

*(***SANDRA*** enters.)*

SANDRA. Jennifer – haven't seen you for ages.

JENNIFER. What are you doing here?

SANDRA. I'm like you – too early for the party. It's always so shaming to be early, isn't it?

JENNIFER. What's this about a party? Whose party?

SANDRA. Well, not a party exactly. The Torrances just said come in for drinks.

JENNIFER. *(Surprised.)* They asked you in for drinks *today*?

SANDRA. Why not? *(Sharply.)* Isn't that why you're here?

JENNIFER. Not exactly.

(She turns away, amused.)

SANDRA. Why shouldn't the Torrances ask me in for drinks?

JENNIFER. No reason at all –

(She pauses.)

– if they'd been in England.

SANDRA. Do you mean they're not in England?

JENNIFER. *(Nodding.)* They're at Juan.

SANDRA. But Pat Torrance rang me up on Tuesday, the day before yesterday.

JENNIFER. *(Mockingly.)* Did she?

SANDRA. *(Sharply.)* Yes.

JENNIFER. *(Coolly.)* Oh, really, darling! You must do better than that. It's never any good sticking to a story that won't gel.

SANDRA. Really, Jennifer!

JENNIFER. *(Laughing.)* I suppose you got Pat Torrance to lend you the key of the flat.

(She eyes her keenly.)

And you're meeting someone here! Who is it? You might tell me. Or shall I try and guess?

SANDRA. You're talking absolute nonsense. I told you, Pat Torrance rang me and asked me to come –

JENNIFER. Oh, darling! Not all over again! Think of something better.

(She looks at the cage.)

Perhaps she asked you to come in and feed the budgerigar?

SANDRA. *(Doubtfully.)* As a matter of fact – she – she did mention –

JENNIFER. *(Laughing.)* But I'd already agreed to feed the little brute for her.

(She takes a packet out of her bag and reads the label.)

"Lov-a-bud Budgie Food. Your Budgie will simply love it."

(She looks mockingly at **SANDRA.***)*

How forgetful of Pat to ask two of us to do the same thing.

SANDRA. *(Angrily.)* Oh, really, Jennifer...

JENNIFER. Oh, don't be cross. I'm only teasing. It's so lovely, catching one's friends out. But you might just tell me who he is. I swear I'll be as silent as the grave.

SANDRA. That'll be the day!

JENNIFER. Now, don't lose your temper, sweetie. What really surprises me is that the Torrances should aid and abet. I've always found them rather straight laced. I put it down to living abroad so much in remote outposts of what used to be Empire. *(Coaxingly.)* Sweetie, do tell me who it is you're having an affair with.

SANDRA. I'm not having an affair with anyone.

JENNIFER. Then why are you here in the Torrances flat when they're in the south of France – telling silly fibs about a cocktail party?

SANDRA. There must have been some mix up or other. You know how things are on the telephone. Perhaps Pat meant next week. But I can tell you that I came here expecting to find a party and that's all there is to it.

JENNIFER. *(Disappointed.)* And you're really and truly not expecting to meet anyone here?

SANDRA. The only person I'm actually expecting to meet here is John.

JENNIFER. Your husband?

SANDRA. Yes. He said he'd join me here as soon as he could get away from the office.

JENNIFER. Dear John. Such a pet, isn't he?

SANDRA. *(Smiling.)* Naturally I think so.

JENNIFER. Such a nice, simple, *trusting* man! He simply worships you, doesn't he?

SANDRA. He doesn't actually dislike me.

JENNIFER. What splendid understatement! Men don't usually dislike you, do they? Quite the contrary.

SANDRA. *(Coldly.)* Hadn't you better feed the budgerigar if that's really what you've come for?

JENNIFER. Sandra! Are you suggesting that I came here to meet someone?

SANDRA. Certainly not! I should never dream of such a thing.

JENNIFER. Well, that really is a bitchy thing to say!

(She moves to the cage, takes the feeding tray out and begins to fill it.)

Tweet, tweet, tweet, here you are, then! Luv-a-bud for the budgie. You know, there's something rather non-U about a budgie, don't you agree? But then there's something terribly non-U about the Torrances. All this travelling about to strange places and bringing back souvenirs. I stole an ashtray from the Carlton in Cannes once, but I never forgave myself.

(She puts the filled seed tray back in the cage.)

And why only one bird, why not two? Look at the poor little mite, all shut up in one room and simply pining for a mate.

(She looks at **SANDRA.***)*

But then, if there were two of you, you'd have to be faithful, wouldn't you? Such a bore. My God, he's drunk his own weight in water since this morning. Never mind, Mother will get you some more. Or do you suppose he'd rather have gin? If it is a he! How do you tell?

(She removes the water dish then exits down the hallway to the kitchen. **SANDRA** *goes out onto the terrace.* **JENNIFER** *re-enters and replaces the water dish in the cage.)*

What are you doing out there, darling? No good looking for the Torrances. I tell you they're abroad. Or perhaps you weren't looking for the Torrances. Well, that's my chore done for the day and I'm going. Goodbye, Sandra.

*(***SANDRA** *re-enters.)*

SANDRA. I'll come with you. No point in my staying, obviously.

JENNIFER. But what about John? He'll be coming.

SANDRA. Oh, John – well, he can –

(The buzzer sounds.)

JENNIFER. I expect that's him now.

(She crosses and opens the front door. **DAVID FORRESTER** *enters. He is a good looking man in his late thirties. Behind his charm and manner you sense a certain ruthlessness. An ambitious man. On seeing the women he looks taken aback but quickly masks his surprise.* **SANDRA** *on the other hand, displays real astonishment.)*

DAVID. Hullo, Sandra.

SANDRA. David!

JENNIFER. Hullo!

DAVID. Hullo.

SANDRA. Er – Mr. Forrester – Mrs. Brice.

*(***JENNIFER** *offers her hand.* **DAVID** *takes it.)*

JENNIFER. How do you do?

DAVID. How do you do?

SANDRA. *(Quickly.)* You seem to have come on the wrong day David, like me. Jennifer has just been telling me the Torrances are abroad.

DAVID. Really.

(He smiles at **JENNIFER**.*)*

That seems to make three of us.

JENNIFER. Oh, I just came in to feed the budgerigar.

*(***DAVID** *looks at the bird.)*

DAVID. *(Vaguely.)* Oh, I see. Nice little fellow. Does he talk?

JENNIFER. Only Swahili.

DAVID. Very expressive language, I've always understood.

JENNIFER. Well, I must fly. So nice to have seen you.

(She looks towards **SANDRA** *maliciously.)*

Goodbye, darling.

*(**JENNIFER** exits through the front door. There is a pause. **DAVID** and **SANDRA** look awkward. **JENNIFER** re-enters.)*

Give my love to John, won't you? It's all been the greatest fun.

(She exits again, closing the door.)

DAVID. Who the devil was that?

SANDRA. Jennifer Brice.

DAVID. Friend of yours?

SANDRA. I wouldn't say so.

DAVID. What was she doing here?

SANDRA. You heard her. She came to feed the budgerigar. Whatever are you doing here?

DAVID. Darling, I came to see you.

SANDRA. Me?

*(**DAVID** looks around the flat.)*

DAVID. By the way, whose flat are we in?

SANDRA. The Torrances.

DAVID. *(Enlightened.)* Oh, I see. Well, it's very nice and suitable.

(He looks at the divan.)

Do both the Torrances sleep on this? Surely not.

SANDRA. I think it opens into a double.

DAVID. That's kind of it.

(There is an awkward pause.)

Sandra...

(He moves to her, they kiss passionately.)

SANDRA. David.

DAVID. It's been quite a while.

SANDRA. Too long!

(They kiss again.)

DAVID. All of a week!

SANDRA. No. Monday, at the theatre.

DAVID. That wasn't what I meant. Has it been long for you, too?

SANDRA. An age. I wish we didn't have to be so secretive.

DAVID. Well, we do.

SANDRA. All this plotting and planning. It's such a bore.

DAVID. It won't always be like this, but just for now. That woman, damned awkward her butting in like that. What does she think?

SANDRA. About us?

DAVID. Yes.

SANDRA. Well, I'm afraid...

DAVID. She'll go away and talk, eh? What damned bad luck. We've been so careful up to now.

SANDRA. I told her I was expecting John to pick me up here.

DAVID. Did she believe you?

SANDRA. *(Dryly.)* She might have done if you hadn't walked in.

DAVID. As I said, damned bad luck.

(He looks out at the terrace.)

I must say you did a very good job of looking surprised.

SANDRA. But I was surprised.

DAVID. How could you be, when you'd asked me to come?

SANDRA. I didn't ask you to come.

DAVID. You didn't?

SANDRA. No.

DAVID. But I got a message.

SANDRA. What message?

DAVID. Would I meet Mrs. Grey at five hundred and thirteen Alberry Mansions at six-thirty. This is Alberry Mansions, isn't it?

SANDRA. Of course it is.

DAVID. Well, then?

(There is a pause.)

SANDRA. David there's something very queer about all this. The Torrances rang up and asked me to come here for drinks.

DAVID. Here we go again. Who are the Torrances?

SANDRA. Michael and Pat. Just come home from the Middle East or Africa or somewhere. United Nations, UNESCO, that sort of thing.

*(**DAVID** looks round at the ornaments.)*

DAVID. Obviously. All the right trappings. So the Torrances rang you up and asked you for drinks – and you came. Obviously it's the wrong day. No signs of preparation for a party.

(He is struck by a sudden idea.)

How did you get in?

SANDRA. I rang and then I found the door wasn't locked. The catch on the Yale was down.

*(**DAVID** crosses to the door and examines the lock.)*

DAVID. So it is. That's peculiar.

SANDRA. It's very peculiar. And the most peculiar thing of all is that the Torrances went to the south of France last Saturday, so how on earth could Pat Torrance ring me up the day before yesterday?

DAVID. She rang you up herself? It wasn't a message?

SANDRA. No, it was Pat. At least I thought it was.

DAVID. But now you're not so sure? Did you recognise her voice?

SANDRA. I don't know her awfully well. She said, "Pat Torrance speaking." It never occurred to me that it wasn't her.

DAVID. There's something behind all this that I don't understand.

SANDRA. I don't either. And I don't like it.

DAVID. But what's the point of it all? Ringing you up, pretending to be Pat Torrance, getting you to come here, getting me to come here by sending me a message, supposedly from you. What does it all add up to?

SANDRA. I wonder –

(She breaks off. **DAVID** *looks at her keenly.)*

DAVID. You've got some idea about it. Come on, tell me.

SANDRA. *(Slowly.)* I wondered if – it might not be – John

DAVID. *(Astonished.)* John?

SANDRA. Sometimes I've thought that he'd begun to suspect about us.

DAVID. *(Sharply.)* You never told me.

SANDRA. I thought I was probably imagining it.

DAVID. *(Thoughtfully.)* John. But how would he tie up with the Torrances? Could he have got this Torrance woman to ring you up and –

SANDRA. That's absurd. John hardly knows her.

DAVID. He might have managed to borrow their flat and then got someone or other to ring up and pretend to be Patricia Torrance.

SANDRA. But why? Why?

DAVID. My dear girl, use your head. To catch us in the act. *In flagrante delicto.*

SANDRA. Oh, I see.

DAVID. Perhaps he's got a couple of bowler-hatted private detectives hiding in the bathroom.

*(**DAVID** exits down the hall then re-enters.)*

Couldn't even hide a bowler hat in there and this place is as bare as your hand. Probably means to come here himself and surprise us in amorous play!

SANDRA. What a beastly, disgusting thing to do!

DAVID. *(Amused.)* No good taking such a high and moral tone, darling. After all, a husband is justified, I suppose, in being annoyed if he finds his wife has taken a lover. How long have you been married now?

SANDRA. Three years.

DAVID. And old John is still inclined to be on the jealous side, eh?

SANDRA. Of course he's jealous, you know that. But on the other hand he's frightfully simple. Anyone could deceive him. I was quite sure he hadn't got a clue until just lately.

DAVID. Well, I suppose some kind friend has been around and told him the good news. Though I must say we've always been careful enough.

SANDRA. *(Bitterly.)* Somebody always knows.

DAVID. Yes. Well, in that case I think the best thing to be done is for us to beat a hasty retreat. We'll meet at the usual place tomorrow, but be sure you're not followed. We certainly can't risk anyone – get your things.

(The buzzer sounds. They freeze.)

SANDRA. *(Quietly.)* Who do you think?

DAVID. Ssh!

(He crosses to **SANDRA**.*)*

If it's John and he doesn't hear anything he'll go away again.

(The buzzer sounds again.)

SANDRA. The door. It's open!

DAVID. I wish I'd put the damned catch down.

(He seats **SANDRA** *on the divan.)*

For God's sake try to relax. Here, have a cigarette.

(He offers her a cigarette from his case.)

Go on!

*(***SANDRA** *takes one.* **DAVID** *lights it then takes one for himself. He moves away and tries to look casual.* **ALEC** *enters. He is a young man of twenty-eight or nine, effeminate, very elegant, amusing, inclined to be spiteful. He*

has a very artificial manner and is dressed in the height of fashion, even wearing gloves.)

Alec!

ALEC. Hullo, David. Hullo, Sandra. Darlings, how devastating. We three seem to be much too early for the party.

SANDRA. *(Relieved.)* There is a party, then? We were just wondering.

ALEC. Yes, it doesn't look much like it, does it? No *canapés,* no baked meats, no olives. I suppose the party is here? The Torrances aren't giving it somewhere else, are they?

DAVID. Well – well – we wondered.

ALEC. How long have you two been here?

SANDRA. *(Quickly.)* Oh, I came about five minutes ago and David has just arrived.

ALEC. Oh, I see. You didn't come together.

SANDRA & DAVID. *(Together.)* No.

*(**ALEC** looks at them. There is a pause.)*

SANDRA. Pat rang you, did she?

ALEC. No, it was Michael as a matter of fact. Of course, he is rather a vague chap. I don't know him all that well. He just said would I roll along here to drinks 6:30 p.m. onwards. So here I am.

DAVID. All dressed up!

ALEC. Well, I've been to the garden party. My dear, the people nowadays!

(He looks around.)

Anyway, I gathered this was to be quite a do.

DAVID. Did Michael say so?

ALEC. No, he just said "drinks" but there are ways of saying things.

(He opens a cabinet and takes out an almost empty bottle of whisky.)

Well, there's something. I'm sure he'd want us to celebrate. Oh!

(He replaces it and brings out a gin bottle.)

Ah, gin! All right? There seems to be tonic.

SANDRA. Fine.

*(**ALEC** pours out three gin and tonics.)*

DAVID. *(Decisively.)* Well, it seems to be quite clear what's happened. The Torrances *are* giving a party but they're giving it somewhere else and either they thought we knew where they were giving it or they forgot to say.

ALEC. It's rather queer though, isn't it?

*(**DAVID** crosses to **SANDRA** with two glasses.)*

I mean, that they should have forgotten to say so to all three of us.

(He holds up his drink.)

Well, "absent friends" seems the right toast. To the Torrances!

DAVID. The Torrances!

*(They drink. **SANDRA** speaks with elaborate pretence.)*

SANDRA. Somebody – it was Jennifer Brice, as a matter of fact, said that the Torrances were abroad. I didn't believe her, but now I wonder.

ALEC. Jennifer Brice! Has she been here?

SANDRA. She came to feed the –

DAVID. Budgerigar.

ALEC. *(Happily.)* My dears, how intriguing. Now wait a minute, let me work it all out. The Torrances have gone away. Somebody else, we don't know who, has asked us three to come here.

*(He turns to **DAVID**.)*

But why? Exciting, isn't it? Quite like one of those mysteries in books. Perhaps they'll expect us to hunt round for a clue, you know, that'll send us on to the next place. Yes.

(He looks round the room.)

Really, what extraordinary things the Torrances have!

(He picks up a coffee pot.)

I suppose they brought this back with them from Baghdad. Oh, what a strange nose it's got.

SANDRA. Yes, cruel.

(He replaces the pot.)

ALEC. Darling, that's very penetrating of you. Yes, it is cruel. It's odd isn't it, but this whole flat looks rather cruel to me. So bare and cold. These four walls that hold you in and just the minimum of necessities to live in it. What a horrible place to be shut up in if you couldn't get out.

DAVID. It's a perfectly ordinary modern flat, Alec. Now don't start thinking up things.

ALEC. You're so hearty, David. You won't let me have any pleasant imaginings.

(He crosses to the chest.)

Now this, I believe, is what is known as a Damascus bride chest. Seems to have worm in it.

(He takes the Kurdish knife and removes its sheath.)

Ough! Here's one of those bloodthirsty knives that you stab your wife with when she's been unfaithful.

(He crosses to **DAVID** *with it.)*

The inlay on the hilt's rather nice, isn't it David? Well, go on. Take it. It won't bite you.

*(***DAVID** *takes the knife briefly before handing it back.)*

DAVID. Yes, splendid.

ALEC. You're so inartistic.

(He turns to **SANDRA** *and gives her the knife.)*

Don't you think it's nice, Sandra?

SANDRA. Beautiful.

(She hands it back to **ALEC** *who then goes out on to the balcony.)*

ALEC. Now, what's out here?

(He turns and looks back at **SANDRA.***)*

Five floors up. What a drop. Might be a cliff in Cornwall. Perfect for suicide. Oh, I've dropped it!

(He re-enters.)

The knife – I've dropped it. Not on anyone's head, fortunately. Now I suppose I'll have to go down and pick it up. What a bore. While I'm there I'll see if I can find a porter.

SANDRA. I don't think there is one.

ALEC. Well, there's an office. There must be a manager or manageress. I'll just pop in and find out if the Torrances are away and if they've let this flat to anyone.

DAVID. We might as well all go.

ALEC. No. You stay here, finish your drinks. Make yourself at home. I shan't be long.

*(***ALEC** *exits through the front door, locking it behind him.)*

DAVID. *(Angrily.)* Of course that ass would turn up here. He's got the most malicious tongue in London.

SANDRA. D'you think he thought it odd, the two of us being here together?

DAVID. I bet he did. He'll probably go around everywhere telling people that we've got the Torrances to lend us their flat to meet in while they're away.

SANDRA. We'd better go.

DAVID. No, wait a minute. If we go off together it looks bad. Isn't Alec rather a friend of John's?

SANDRA. Oh, in a way. The person Alec was really devoted to was my first husband, Barry. He was really terribly upset when Barry died.

DAVID. When he went over that cliff in Cornwall?

SANDRA. Yes. *(Amused.)* With the fuss Alec made anyone would think I'd pushed Barry over.

DAVID. *(Lightly.)* Did you?

SANDRA. What do you mean?

DAVID. Nothing.

SANDRA. I jolly nearly went over myself. *(Shivering.)* It was terrifying. The whole cliff subsided after a heavy rain.

DAVID. *(Thoughtfully.)* So Alec doesn't like you very much.

SANDRA. I don't think he likes any women.

DAVID. But he particularly doesn't like you?

SANDRA. What are you getting at?

DAVID. I just wondered if it could be Alec who's behind this whole thing. Getting us here, I mean.

SANDRA. But why should he?

DAVID. Getting us to meet here and then passing the word to John to come and find us together.

SANDRA. That's ridiculous. Anyway, if Alec had done that, why should he come here himself? That would ruin the whole point of the thing.

DAVID. Yes, yes, you're right. At any rate, we might as well get out of here now. We'll go and join friend Alec down below.

SANDRA. I must say I'd like to know the explanation of all this, it does seems so queer. I can't really believe that –

(**DAVID** *rattles the handle to the front door.)*

DAVID. Hullo, this door's locked.

SANDRA. Oh, I expect the latch has slipped back in the Yale.

(**DAVID** *turns the Yale lock.)*

DAVID. No, no, it's not the Yale. You see there's another lock below. A mortice lock. *That* seems to be locked.

SANDRA. But it can't be. We got in quite easily –

DAVID. Somebody seems to have locked it from the outside.

SANDRA. Locked us in, do you mean?

DAVID. Yes.

SANDRA. But that's absurd. We can –

(She stops.)

Who locked it?

DAVID. Alec.

SANDRA. Alec? Why should Alec lock us in?

(She moves to the door.)

All we have to do is bang or shout.

DAVID. No, don't do that. Wait a minute, sit down. We've got to think this out first. There's something very odd going on. It may be Alec or it may be someone else. *Somebody* got us here, pretending to you to be the Torrances and sending me a message apparently from you. Whoever it is got us here and now we're locked up here, together.

SANDRA. But it's absurd. We've only got to shout.

DAVID. Oh yes, shout. And then what happens? A scandal. Here we are, meeting in somebody else's flat while they're away, obviously a guilty assignation of some kind and then some practical joker has locked us in.

SANDRA. Then the sooner we call his bluff the better. We'll make a hell of a row and pass it all off as a joke.

(**DAVID***'s manner starts to get unpleasant.)*

DAVID. I tell you I can't afford a scandal! It'll absolutely ruin my chances of getting that appointment. If John were to bring divorce proceedings now, it'd be the end.

SANDRA. What a selfish brute you are. You don't think of anyone but yourself. What about me? What about my reputation?

DAVID. You've never had much of one.

(**SANDRA** *slaps him.)*

(Quietly.) Sit down.

(She does so.)

Let me think. Yes. Somebody laid a trap for us and we're caught in it. We've got to think of the best way out.

SANDRA. You still think it was John. I don't believe it.

DAVID. It's Alec I'm thinking of. Alec hates my guts, always has. Suppose that Alec worked upon John and –

(He stops abruptly, looking down at the ground.)

SANDRA. What is it?

*(**DAVID** kneels at the chest, touching something on the floor.)*

DAVID. Sawdust. A little heap of sawdust. These holes – they're not worm holes. They've been drilled. Four little round holes. Air holes, so that somebody could breathe.

SANDRA. *(Rising.)* What do you mean?

DAVID. Supposing Alec worked on John's suspicions, supposing he suggested that John should hide in the chest and that he, Alec, would arrange to get us here together.

SANDRA. You mean – you mean that John's hiding now in that chest? He is there now? That he's heard all we've been saying – that – that –

DAVID. I think it's possible – quite possible.

*(**DAVID** opens the lid of the chest, looks inside then quickly closes it.)*

My God!

SANDRA. What is it? What is it?

(She moves to the chest.)

DAVID. Don't! Don't look inside!

SANDRA. What is it?

*(**DAVID** takes her and sits her down.)*

DAVID. Come and sit down. Now, don't scream. Keep your voice down. We've got to keep our heads over this.

SANDRA. Tell me.

DAVID. It's John. He's there, in that chest. And he's dead.

(There is a pause.)

SANDRA. Dead? John?

DAVID. He's been killed. Did you do it?

SANDRA. Me? What do you mean?

DAVID. You were here when I came – you sent me a message –

SANDRA. Why should I kill John in a strange flat and ask you to come here?

DAVID. So that I should be in it with you, my dear. You've hinted once or twice that you'd like to marry me and you knew divorce doesn't suit my book.

SANDRA. Do you think I want to get us both hanged for murder?

DAVID. No, you thought we'd get away with it. This is somebody else's flat, isn't it? People who are away. Who was to know that you or I had been here? There's no porter downstairs, no one saw us come in, we've no connection with this place.

SANDRA. I might just as well say that you killed him.

(She rises.)

You came here perhaps, met John, killed him, put him in that chest and then went away, watched for me to arrive and came back.

DAVID. Oh, for God's sake don't talk such rot. The trouble with you is that you're so damnably stupid.

SANDRA. *(Furiously.)* You're saying what you really think now, aren't you? None of your famous charm. You're a louse, that's what you are, a louse and a rat!

DAVID. What about you? How many men have you hopped into bed with, I should like to know?

SANDRA. You bastard! You filthy, rotten bastard!

(The telephone rings. There is a pause.)

Who – who do you think it is?

DAVID. I don't know.

SANDRA. Should we?

DAVID. I think – not.

SANDRA. It may be just Alec ringing up from downstairs.

*(**DAVID** goes to pick up the telephone.)*

No – don't.

(He turns to her.)

Don't.

DAVID. I can't think. I can't think.

(After a pause he goes to answer it again but the telephone stops.)

SANDRA. If that was Alec, he'll think it very odd won't he?

DAVID. If that's Alec he'll probably come up and see.

(He pauses.)

I don't think it was Alec.

SANDRA. Who do you think it was?

DAVID. I don't know. I don't know. I've got to think – we've got to think clearly. Somebody got us here, somebody got John here. Somebody's locked us in from outside. Alec. It must be Alec.

(He goes to the chest and lifts the lid. Struck by an idea he quickly closes it and goes out on to the balcony.)

SANDRA. What are you doing?

*(**DAVID** re-enters.)*

DAVID. D'you remember that Kurdish knife that Alec dropped over the balcony? He said he was going downstairs to pick it up.

SANDRA. What about it?

DAVID. Well, he didn't pick it up. It's still down there.

SANDRA. I don't understand.

DAVID. John was stabbed with that knife.

(There is a pause.)

Don't you see? The pattern's getting pretty plain.

SANDRA. *(Wildly.)* I don't see. I don't see anything. It's like a nightmare.

DAVID. There's only one person behind this. Alec. He told John that we two had arranged to meet here and he suggested that John should bore some air holes in that chest and hide inside it. Then he stabbed John and left him there. He went away and watched for us to arrive and then he came back. He drew our attention to that knife. He had his gloves on the whole time, you remember, he gave it to me to hold, made me take it. Then you took it. Don't you understand? Our fingerprints are on that knife and there isn't a damn thing we can do about it. Then he went away and locked the door, locking us in with a murdered man. Two people who've the best motives in the world for murdering him.

SANDRA. But that's crazy – crazy.

DAVID. Your fingerprints and mine on the knife, nobody else's. And there's not a damned thing we can do but wait for the police to arrive.

SANDRA. The police? Why should the police arrive?

DAVID. Don't you see that logically that's bound to be the next thing that happens, the next stage in Alec's plan?

SANDRA. Alec must be mad – mad. Why should he do this to us?

DAVID. You said he was devoted to your first husband, Barry. You've only got to take one look at Alec to see what kind of devotion that was.

SANDRA. Well? What's that got to do with John?

DAVID. Did you push Barry over that cliff?

SANDRA. Of course I didn't. I told you I –

*(**DAVID** grabs **SANDRA**.)*

DAVID. Listen Sandra, I don't care a damn whether you pushed him over or not. But we've got to have this in the clear because we've got to know Alec's reason. Did you? You were in love with John then weren't you, but he was a straight, simple type. Barry was a rich man, John was poor. Divorce wouldn't have suited you. You were out on that cliff together, you and Barry, and the landslide happened. You saw your chance and you pushed Barry over.

(He shakes her.)

Didn't you? Didn't you?

*(**SANDRA**, very vaguely, finally nods her head.)*

And Alec knew!

SANDRA. He couldn't have known.

DAVID. Alec knew his people. He not only suspected, he was sure. He bided his time. You married John then you got tired of him and started an affair with me. Then Alec saw his chance. To punish, as he'd put it, John and you and me. Mad of course, he's mad. The question is what are we going to do now?

SANDRA. We've got to get out of here.

DAVID. Of course we've got to get out of here, but how?

SANDRA. We can beat on the door. We can shout.

DAVID. What the hell good will that do us? Somebody will come and let us out, then they'll find the body and there we shall be. Hauled in for murder and a defence so fantastic no counsel would listen to it. My God, you even told that Brice woman you were *expecting* to meet John here.

SANDRA. But we'll say Alec was here, we'll explain...

DAVID. Idiot! Alec will simply deny the whole thing. He had his gloves on every moment he was here. He'll deny ever having been near the place. Probably got a very pretty little alibi cooked up somewhere.

SANDRA. Somebody must have seen him come here?

DAVID. In a rabbit warren like this? I doubt it. Some way out – there must be some way out.

*(**DAVID** exits down the hallway to the kitchen and bathroom. **SANDRA** moves slowly to the chest, she is about to open it when **DAVID** re-enters.)*

Two damned square hygienic little boxes!

(He goes out on to the balcony then re-enters.)

SANDRA. Isn't there a fire escape?

DAVID. In the corridor outside, I dare say. From here there's nothing but a sheer drop. There must be some way – some way.

SANDRA. The telephone! We could ring someone up. We could say –

DAVID. Yes, yes! Why the hell didn't I think of that before?

(He stops.)

Who could we ring up? What could we say?

(The telephone rings. There is a pause.)

SANDRA. Answer it! For God's sake answer it. It can't be worse than this.

DAVID. Yes. Yes, I think you're right there.

(He picks up the telephone, adopting a rather different voice.)

Hullo?

*(He puts his hand over the telephone and turns to **SANDRA**.)*

It's Alec.

SANDRA. Alec?

*(**DAVID** listens. A voice can be heard, but not what it says. He stands frozen a moment then puts the telephone down.)*

What is it? What did he say?

DAVID. He said we were caught like rats in a trap, like the rats we are. He said that in three or four minutes the police would be arriving.

SANDRA. Police!

(She looks out over the balcony.)

Police! No, no. There must be some way out.

DAVID. There's only one way out. Through that window and down.

SANDRA. Suicide? You're mad. They'll believe what we say, we'll explain –

DAVID. We'll be charged with murder. We'll be convicted.

SANDRA. No!

(She looks towards the front door. There is a fanlight above it.)

There must be some way out, there must.

(She goes to the coffee table and sweeps it clear. Taking it to the front door she stands on it and puts a hand through the fanlight.)

DAVID. What are you trying to do you little fool? Claw your way out! Claw your way out!

*(**SANDRA** climbs off the table and faces **DAVID**.)*

SANDRA. I didn't do it. I didn't kill John. It's all your fault. Why did I ever meet you? Why didn't you leave me alone?

DAVID. You bloody little bitch, you got me into this.

SANDRA. I hate the sight of you. I tell you I hate the sight of you. You're cold and hard and cruel and selfish as sin. You've never given a damn for anyone in the world except yourself.

*(**DAVID** grabs her throat savagely. There is a knocking at the front door.)*

VOICE. Open the door. It's the police.

*(**DAVID** releases her.)*

DAVID. Let them do it.

(He turns to **SANDRA.***)*

You got away with it the first time, didn't you? But you won't get away with it this time.

(The knocking is repeated.)

VOICE. Come on! Open up!

SANDRA. I hate you.

DAVID. Or perhaps it'll be fifteen years in a prison cell. And how will you care for that? Fifteen years in a prison cell.

VOICE. We'll break the door down.

DAVID. Why should they come for me? It's you they should be coming for, not me. You killed Barry, not me. Why the hell should I get involved?

(The knocking turns into a solid banging as the police attempt to break down the door. **SANDRA** *laughs hysterically.)*

SANDRA. Rats in a trap, that's what we are. Rats in a trap.

End of Play

The Patient

CHARACTERS

LANSEN
NURSE
DR GINSBERG
INSPECTOR CRAY
BRYAN WINGFIELD
EMMELINE ROSS
WILLIAM ROSS
BRENDA JACKSON

THE PATIENT was first presented by Peter Saunders at the Duchess Theatre, London on 29 December 1962. The director was Hubert Gregg, with sets by Peter Rice. The cast was as follows:

LANSEN .... Raymond Bowers
NURSE .... Mercy Haystead
DR. GINSBERG .... Robert Raglan
INSPECTOR CRAY .... David Langhn
BRYAN WINGFIELD .... Michael Beint
EMMELINE ROSS .... Vera Cook
WILLIAM ROSS .... Robin May
BRENDA JACKSON .... Betty McDowall
THE PATIENT .... Rosemary Martin

(A private room in a nursing home. The room is plain and hygienic looking. There is a set of double doors leading to other parts of the nursing home and across the back a large window covered by Venetian blinds which are at present down but not closed. There is also a small alcove which currently has a curtain drawn across it. There is a piece of electrical apparatus with dials and a red light, a hospital trolley with a steriliser on top and a wall telephone with a bell next to it. There is also a small table with an elbow chair next to it and four small chairs in a rough semicircle. These chairs have the appearance of having been brought into the room for a purpose and not really belonging to it. **LANSEN**, *a tall gangling young man with spectacles, wearing a long white hospital overall, is fiddling with the electrical apparatus. The* **NURSE**, *a tall, good looking woman, competent and correct, is at the trolley. She lifts the lid of the steriliser, removes a needle with some forceps then places it on a tray. Crossing to the alcove she draws back the curtain, takes out a towel and crosses back to the trolley. A buzzer sounds.* **DR. GINSBERG** *enters through the double doors. He is a dark, clever looking man in his middle forties. He makes for the telephone.)*

GINSBERG. All right, Nurse, I'll answer it.

(He picks up the telephone.)

Yes? ... Oh, Inspector Cray, good. Ask him to come up to Room Fourteen, will you?

(He puts down the telephone and crosses to **LANSEN** *and the electrical apparatus.)*

GINSBERG. How are you doing, Lansen? Got it fixed up?

LANSEN. Yes, everything's in order. I'll plug in here, Dr. Ginsberg.

GINSBERG. You're quite sure about this, now? We can't afford to have a slip up.

LANSEN. Quite sure, Doctor. It'll work a treat.

GINSBERG. Good.

(He turns and looks at the chairs.)

Oh, a little less formal I think, Nurse. Let's move these chairs a bit.

(He moves one to the corner.)

Er – that one over there against the wall.

NURSE. Yes, Doctor.

*(***GINSBERG** *exits. The* **NURSE** *lifts a chair, taking it passed the electrical apparatus.)*

LANSEN. Careful!

(He takes it from her and places it against the wall. The **NURSE** *indicates the apparatus with slight curiosity.)*

NURSE. What is this thing?

LANSEN. *(Grinning.)* New electrical gadget.

NURSE. *(Bored.)* Oh, one of those.

LANSEN. Trouble with you people is you've no respect for science.

*(***INSPECTOR CRAY** *enters. He is a middle-aged man of delusively mild appearance.* **GINSBERG** *follows.)*

INSPECTOR. Good afternoon.

GINSBERG. Everything's ready.

(The **INSPECTOR** *indicates the apparatus.)*

INSPECTOR. Is this the contraption?

LANSEN. Good afternoon, Inspector.

GINSBERG. Yes. It's been well tested, Inspector.

LANSEN. It works perfectly. The least touch will make a connection. I guarantee there will be no hitch.

GINSBERG. All right, Lansen. We'll call you when we need you.

(**LANSEN** *exits.* **GINSBERG** *turns to the* **NURSE.**)

Has Nurse Cartwright got the patient ready?

NURSE. Yes, Doctor. Quite ready.

GINSBERG. Nurse Bond here is going to stay and assist me during the experiment.

INSPECTOR. Oh, good. That's very kind of you.

NURSE. Not at all, Inspector. I'll do anything I can to help. I'd never have gone off duty if I'd thought that Mrs. Wingfield was unduly depressed.

GINSBERG. Nobody's blaming you, Nurse.

(He turns to the **INSPECTOR.**)

You say the others have arrived?

INSPECTOR. Yes, they're downstairs.

GINSBERG. All four of them?

INSPECTOR. All four of them. Bryan Wingfield, Emmeline Ross, William Ross and Brenda Jackson. They can't leave, I've posted my men.

GINSBERG. *(Formally.)* You must understand Inspector, that the well-being of my patient comes before anything else. At the first sign of collapse or undue excitement, any indication that the experiment is having an adverse effect, I shall stop the proceedings.

(He turns to the **NURSE.**)

You understand that, Nurse?

NURSE. Yes, Doctor.

INSPECTOR. Quite so, quite so, I shouldn't expect anything else. *(Uneasily.)* You don't think it's too risky?

GINSBERG. *(Coldly.)* If I thought it was too risky I should not permit the experiment. Mrs. Wingfield's condition is mainly psychological, the result of severe shock. Her temperature, heart and pulse are now normal. Nurse, you are already acquainted with the family. Go down to the waiting room and bring them up here. If they ask you any questions please be strictly non-committal in your answers.

NURSE. Yes, Doctor.

(The **NURSE** *exits.)*

INSPECTOR. Well, here we go.

GINSBERG. Yes.

INSPECTOR. Let's hope we have luck. Have any of them been allowed to see her?

GINSBERG. Her husband, naturally. And also her brother and sister for a few minutes. The nurse assigned to look after her here, Nurse Cartwright, was present all the time.

(He pauses.)

Miss Jackson has not visited Mrs. Wingfield, nor asked to do so.

INSPECTOR. Quite so. You'll give them a little preliminary talk, will you? Put them in the picture.

GINSBERG. Certainly, if you wish. I see that Mrs. Wingfield fell from the second storey balcony.

INSPECTOR. Yes. Yes, she did.

GINSBERG. Remarkable really, that she wasn't killed. Head contusions, dislocated shoulder and fracture of the left leg.

(The **NURSE** *enters. She holds a door open and* **BRYAN WINGFIELD, WILLIAM ROSS,** *and* **EMMELINE ROSS** *enter.* **WINGFIELD** *is a short, stocky man of about thirty-five, attractive, with a quiet manner and a poker face.* **ROSS** *is a man of the same age, also short, but dark-haired, rather mercurial in temperament.*

EMMELINE, *his sister, is a tall, grim faced woman of forty. They are all in a state of emotional disturbance. The* **NURSE** *exits.* **GINSBERG** *shakes hands with them in turn.)*

Good afternoon, Miss Ross, will you sit down?

(She does so. He turns to **ROSS** *and finally* **WINGFIELD**.*)*

Mr. Ross! Good afternoon. Mr. Wingfield.

WINGFIELD. You sent for us – it's not – my wife? There's not bad news?

GINSBERG. No, Mr. Wingfield. No bad news.

WINGFIELD. Thank God. When you sent for us I thought there might be a change for the worse.

GINSBERG. There is no change of any kind, neither for the worse nor, alas, for the better.

EMMELINE. Is my sister still unconscious?

GINSBERG. She is still completely paralysed. She cannot move or speak.

EMMELINE. It's terrible. Simply terrible!

INSPECTOR. Was Miss Jackson with you?

WINGFIELD. She was following us.

*(***BRENDA JACKSON** *enters. She is a tall, extremely pretty young woman of twenty-five.)*

Dr. Ginsberg, my secretary, Miss Jackson.

GINSBERG. Good afternoon.

*(***WINGFIELD** *indicates a chair and* **BRENDA** *crosses to it. She eyes the electrical apparatus.)*

ROSS. Poor Jenny, what an awful thing to happen to anyone. Sometimes I feel it would have been better if she'd been killed outright by the fall.

WINGFIELD. No. Anything but that.

ROSS. I know what you feel, Bryan. But this – I mean, it's a living death isn't it, Doctor?

GINSBERG. There's still some hope for your sister, Mr. Ross.

BRENDA. But she won't stay like this? I mean – she'll get better won't she?

GINSBERG. In cases of this kind it is very difficult to forecast the progress of a patient. Her injuries will heal, yes. The bones will knit, the dislocation has already been reduced, the wounds in the head are nearly healed.

WINGFIELD. Then why shouldn't she get well? Why shouldn't she be herself again in every way?

GINSBERG. You are touching there on a field in which we are still ignorant. Mrs. Wingfield's state of paralysis is due to shock.

EMMELINE. The result of her accident?

GINSBERG. Her accident was the ostensible cause.

ROSS. Just what do you mean by ostensible?

GINSBERG. Mrs. Wingfield must have suffered unusual fears before she fell from the balcony. It is not so much her *physical* injuries but something in her *mind* that has produced this state of complete paralysis.

(**BRENDA** *sits.*)

WINGFIELD. You're not trying to say – you're not thinking what I'm sure the Inspector has been more or less suggesting, that my wife tried to commit suicide? That I don't believe for a moment.

INSPECTOR. I haven't said I thought it was suicide, Mr. Wingfield.

WINGFIELD. You must think something of the kind or you and your people wouldn't keep hanging round like vultures.

INSPECTOR. We have to be quite clear as to the cause of this – accident.

ROSS. *(Impatiently.)* My God, isn't it simple enough? She's been ill for months. She'd been feeling weak, up for the first time, or practically the first time. Goes over to the window, out on to the balcony, leans over, is suddenly taken giddy and falls to the ground. That balcony's very low.

EMMELINE. Don't get so excited William, don't shout.

ROSS. It's all very well, Bunny, but it makes me mad all this business.

(He turns to **GINSBERG.***)*

Do you think it's pleasant for us having the police mixing themselves up in our family affairs?

WINGFIELD. Now Bill, if anyone should complain it's myself and I don't.

BRENDA. What have we been asked to come here for?

INSPECTOR. One moment, Miss Jackson.

(He turns to **EMMELINE.***)*

Miss Ross, I wish you could tell me a little more about your sister. Was she at all subject to fits of melancholy – depression?

EMMELINE. She was always highly strung, nervous.

ROSS. Oh, I wouldn't say that at all.

EMMELINE. Men don't realise these things. I know what I'm talking about. I think it is quite possible, Inspector, that her illness had left her particularly low and depressed and that with other things she had to worry and distress her...

*(***BRENDA** *rises and makes to exit. Everyone turns. The* **INSPECTOR** *stops her.)*

INSPECTOR. Where are you going, Miss Jackson?

BRENDA. I'm leaving. I'm not one of the family, I'm only Mr. Wingfield's secretary. I don't see the point of all this. I was asked to come with the others, but if all you're going to do is to go over and over again about the accident – whether it was accident or attempted suicide – well, I don't see why I should stay.

INSPECTOR. But it's not going to be the same thing over and over again, Miss Jackson. We are about to make an experiment.

BRENDA. *(Arrested.)* An experiment? What kind of experiment?

INSPECTOR. Dr. Ginsberg will explain. Sit down, Miss Jackson.

*(**BRENDA** moves back to her chair and sits.)*

Dr. Ginsberg!

GINSBERG. I had better perhaps recapitulate what I know or have been told. Mrs. Wingfield has been suffering in the last two months from an illness somewhat mysterious in nature which was puzzling the doctor in attendance on her, Dr. Horsefield. This I have on the authority of Dr. Horsefield himself. She was however, showing decided signs of improvement and was convalescent, though there was still a nurse in the house. On the day in question, exactly ten days ago, Mrs. Wingfield got up from bed after lunch and was settled by Nurse Bond in an easy chair near the open window, it being a fine, mild afternoon. She had books beside her and a small radio. After seeing her patient had all she needed, Nurse went out for her afternoon walk as usual. What happened during the course of the afternoon is a matter of conjecture. But at half past three a cry was heard. Miss Ross, who was sitting in the room below, saw a falling body cross the window. It was the body of Mrs. Wingfield, who had fallen from the balcony of her room. There was no one with her at the time when she fell but there were four people in the house, the four people who are assembled here now.

INSPECTOR. Perhaps, Mr. Wingfield, you would like to tell us in your own words just what happened then?

WINGFIELD. I should have thought I'd told it often enough already. I was correcting proofs in my study. I heard a scream, a noise from outside. I rushed to the side door, went out on the terrace and found – and found poor Jenny.

(He turns away.)

Emmeline joined me a moment later and then William and Miss Jackson. We telephoned for the doctor and I – I –

(His voice breaks.)

INSPECTOR. Yes, yes, Mr. Wingfield, there's no need to go into any more.

(He turns to **BRENDA.***)*

Miss Jackson, will you tell us again your side of the story?

BRENDA. I had been asked to look up a reference in the encyclopaedia for Mr. Wingfield. I was in the library when I heard a commotion and people running. I dropped the book and came out and joined them on the terrace.

(The **INSPECTOR** *turns to* **ROSS.***)*

INSPECTOR. Mr. Ross?

ROSS. What? Oh – I'd been playing golf all the morning, always play golf on a Saturday. I'd come in, eaten a hearty lunch and was feeling whacked. I lay down on my bed upstairs. It was Jenny's scream that woke me up. I thought for a moment I must have been dreaming. Then I heard the row down below and I looked out of my window. There she was on the terrace with the others gathered round. *(Fiercely.)* Oh God, have we got to go over this again and again?

INSPECTOR. I only wanted to stress the point that nobody who was in the house can tell us exactly what happened that afternoon.

(He pauses.)

Nobody, that is, except Mrs. Wingfield herself.

ROSS. It's all perfectly simple, as I've said all along. Poor Jenny thought she was stronger than she was. She went out on the balcony, leant over, and that's that. Perfectly simple accident, might have happened to anybody.

WINGFIELD. Somebody ought to have been with her. I blame myself for leaving her alone.

EMMELINE. But she was supposed to rest in the afternoon Bryan, that was part of the doctor's orders. We were all going to join her at half past four for tea, but she was supposed to rest every afternoon from three o'clock until then.

INSPECTOR. Miss Ross, the accident seems a little difficult to explain. The railings of the balcony did not give way.

ROSS. No, no. She got giddy and overbalanced. I leant over myself to test it afterwards and it could easily happen.

INSPECTOR. Mrs. Wingfield is a very small woman. It wouldn't be so easy for her to overbalance even if she was taken giddy.

EMMELINE. I hate to say it, but I think you're right in what you suspect. I think poor Jenny was worried and troubled in her mind. I think a fit of depression came over her –

WINGFIELD. You keep saying she tried to commit suicide. I don't believe it. I won't believe it.

EMMELINE. *(Significantly.)* She had plenty to make her depressed.

WINGFIELD. What do you mean by that?

EMMELINE. *(Rising.)* I think you know quite well what I mean. I'm not blind, Bryan.

WINGFIELD. Jenny wasn't depressed. She'd nothing to be depressed about. You've got an evil mind Emmeline and you just imagine things.

ROSS. Leave my sister alone.

*(**BRENDA** rises.)*

BRENDA. It was an accident. Of course it was an accident. Miss Ross is just trying to – trying to –

EMMELINE. Yes, what am I trying to do?

BRENDA. It's women like you that write anonymous letters – poison pen letters. Just because no man has ever looked at you.

EMMELINE. How dare you!

ROSS. Oh my God! Women! Cut it out, both of you.

WINGFIELD. I think we're all rather over excited, you know. We're talking about things that are quite beside the point. What we really want to get at is what was Jenny's state of mind on the day she fell? Well, I'm her husband, I know her pretty well and I don't think for a moment she meant to commit suicide.

EMMELINE. Because you don't want to think so – you don't want to feel responsible!

WINGFIELD. Responsible? What do you mean by responsible?

EMMELINE. Driving her to do what she did!

(Everyone speaks simultaneously.)

ROSS. What do you mean by that?

WINGFIELD. How dare you!

BRENDA. It's not true!

*(**GINSBERG** silences them.)*

GINSBERG. Please – please! When I asked you to come here, it was not my object to provoke recriminations.

ROSS. *(Angrily.)* Wasn't it? I'm not so sure.

*(He looks suspiciously at the **INSPECTOR**.)*

GINSBERG. No, what I had in mind was to conduct an experiment.

BRENDA. We've already been told that, but you still haven't told us what kind of experiment.

GINSBERG. As Inspector Cray said just now, only one person knows what happened that afternoon – Mrs. Wingfield herself.

WINGFIELD. *(Sighing.)* And she can't tell us. It's too bad.

EMMELINE. She will when she's better.

GINSBERG. I don't think you quite appreciate the medical position, Miss Ross.

*(He crosses to the electrical apparatus. **BRENDA** sits.)*

It may be months, it may even be years before Mrs. Wingfield comes out of this state.

WINGFIELD. Surely not.

GINSBERG. Yes, Mr. Wingfield. I won't go into a lot of medical details, but there are people who have gone blind as a result of shock and have not recovered their sight for fifteen or twenty years. There have been those paralysed and unable to walk for the same periods of time. Sometimes another shock precipitates recovery. But there's no fixed rule.

(He turns to the **INSPECTOR**.*)*

Ring the bell, please.

(The **INSPECTOR** *crosses and rings the bell.)*

WINGFIELD. I don't quite understand what you are driving at Doctor.

(He looks from **GINSBERG** *to the* **INSPECTOR**.*)*

INSPECTOR. You're about to find out, Mr. Wingfield.

*(***GINSBERG** *crosses to the window and closes the Venetian blinds. The lights dim.)*

GINSBERG. Inspector, do you mind?

(The **INSPECTOR** *switches on the lights.* **LANSEN** *opens the doors and pulls on a trolley carrying the* **PATIENT**. *The* **NURSE** *follows. The* **PATIENT***'s head is heavily bandaged, nothing of the features show but the eyes and nose. Her eyes are open but she is quite motionless.)*

WINGFIELD. Jenny, darling!

*(***WINGFIELD** *moves to her side.* **LANSEN** *collects the electrical apparatus and moves it nearer.)*

BRENDA. What's going on? What are you trying to do?

GINSBERG. Mrs. Wingfield, as I have told you, is completely paralysed. She cannot move or speak. But we are all agreed that she knows what happened to her on that day.

BRENDA. She's unconscious. She may be unconscious – oh – for years, you said.

GINSBERG. I did not say unconscious. Mrs. Wingfield cannot move and cannot speak but she *can* see and hear. I think it highly probable that her mind is as keen as ever it was. She knows what happened. She would like to communicate it to us but unfortunately she can't do so.

WINGFIELD. You think she can hear us? You think she does know what we are saying to her, what we're feeling?

GINSBERG. I think she knows.

WINGFIELD. Jenny! Jenny, darling! Can you hear me? It's been terrible for you, I know, but everything's going to be all right.

GINSBERG. Lansen?

(**LANSEN** *is making final adjustments to the electrical apparatus.)*

LANSEN. I'm ready, sir, when you are.

GINSBERG. I said Mrs. Wingfield could not communicate with us but it is possible that a way has been found. Dr. Zalzbergen, who has been attending her and who is a specialist on this form of paralysis, became aware of a very slight power of movement in the fingers of the right hand. It is very slight, hardly noticeable. She could not raise her arm or lift anything but she can very slightly move the two fingers and thumb of her right hand. Mr. Lansen here has fixed up a certain apparatus of an electrical nature.

(**ROSS** *moves closer to the trolley.)*

You see, there is a small rubber bulb. When that bulb is pressed a red light appears on the top of the apparatus. The slightest pressure will operate it. If you please, Lansen!

(**LANSEN** *presses the bulb twice. The red light flashes twice.)*

Nurse, uncover the patient's right arm. Lansen, between the thumb and two fingers. Gently.

(The **NURSE** *lays the* **PATIENT***'s arm on the coverlet.* **LANSEN** *places the bulb in her hand and crosses to the electrical apparatus.)*

GINSBERG. Now I'm going to ask Mrs. Wingfield some questions.

ROSS. Ask her questions? What do you mean? Questions about what?

GINSBERG. Questions about what happened on that Saturday afternoon.

*(***ROSS** *turns to the* **INSPECTOR***.)*

ROSS. This is your doing!

GINSBERG. The experiment was suggested by Mr. Lansen and myself.

WINGFIELD. But you can't possibly put any reliance on what might be purely muscular spasms.

GINSBERG. I think we can soon find out whether Mrs. Wingfield can answer questions or not.

WINGFIELD. I won't have it! It's dangerous for her. It'll set her recovery back. I won't allow this! I won't agree to it.

BRENDA. *(Warningly.)* Bryan!

(She turns to face **WINGFIELD** *then senses the* **INSPECTOR** *watching her and sits.)*

GINSBERG. Mrs. Wingfield's health will be fully safeguarded, I assure you. Nurse!

(The **NURSE** *places her fingers on the* **PATIENT***'s wrist, taking the pulse.)*

At the least sign of collapse, you know what to do.

NURSE. Yes, Doctor.

*(***BRENDA** *speaks almost under her breath.)*

BRENDA. I don't like this – I don't like it.

EMMELINE. I'm sure you don't like it.

BRENDA. Do you?

EMMELINE. I think it might be interesting.

(They speak simultaneously.)

ROSS. I don't believe for a –

WINGFIELD. Inspector, I hope –

INSPECTOR. Quiet, please! We must have absolute quiet. The doctor is about to begin.

(There is a pause.)

GINSBERG. Mrs. Wingfield, you have had a very narrow escape from death and are now on the way to recovery. Your physical injuries are healing. We know that you are paralysed and that you cannot speak or move. What I want is this – if you understand what I am saying to you, try and move your fingers so that you press the bulb. Will you do so?

(There is a pause. The red light comes on. There is a collective gasp. The **INSPECTOR** *now watches them very closely.)*

You have heard and understood what we have been saying, Mrs. Wingfield?

(One red light.)

Thank you. Now what I propose is this: when the answer to a question is "yes" you press the bulb once, if the answer is "no" you will press it twice. Do you understand?

(One red light.)

Now, Mrs. Wingfield, what is the signal for "no"?

(Two red lights in succession.)

I think then, it must be clear to all of you that Mrs. Wingfield can understand what I'm saying and can reply to my questions. I'm going back to the afternoon of Saturday the fourteenth. Have you a clear recollection of what happened that afternoon?

(One red light.)

As far as possible, I will ask you questions that will save you too much fatigue. I am assuming therefore, that you had lunch, got up and that Nurse here settled you in a chair by the window. You were alone in your room with the window open and were supposed to rest until four-thirty. Am I correct?

(One red light.)

Did you in fact, sleep a little?

(One red light.)

And then you woke up?

(One red light.)

Went out on to the balcony?

(One red light.)

You leant over?

(One red light.)

You lost your balance and fell?

(There is a pause. **LANSEN** *bends over to adjust the electrical apparatus.)*

Just a minute, Lansen! You fell?

(One red light.)

But you did not lose your balance.

(Two red lights. A gasp from everyone.)

You were giddy – felt faint?

(Two red lights.)

WINGFIELD. Inspector, I –

INSPECTOR. Sssh!

GINSBERG. Mrs. Wingfield, we have come to the point where you have to tell us what happened. I am going to go over the letters of the alphabet. When I come to the letter of the word you want, will you press the bulb. I'll begin. A, B, C, D, E, F, G, H, I, J, K, L, M, N, O, P.

(One red light.)

You have given me the letter "P." I'm going to hazard a guess – I want you to tell me if I am right. Is the word in your mind "pushed"?

(One red light. There is a general sensation. **BRENDA** *shrinks, her face in her hands.* **ROSS** *swears.* **EMMELINE** *is still.)*

BRENDA. No, it can't be true!

ROSS. What the hell!

WINGFIELD. This is iniquitous!

GINSBERG. Quiet, please. I cannot have the patient agitated. Mrs. Wingfield, you obviously have more to tell us. I'm going to spell again. A, B, C, D, E, F, G, H, I, J, K, L, M.

(One red light.)

M? The letter "M" is probably followed by a vowel. Which vowel, Mrs. Wingfield? A, E, I, O, U.

(One red light. The **INSPECTOR** *moves to the electrical apparatus.)*

M-U?

(One red light.)

Is the next letter "R?"

(One red light. The **INSPECTOR** *and* **GINSBERG** *exchange a look.)*

M-U-R. Mrs. Wingfield, are you trying to tell us that what happened that afternoon was not an accident? Are you trying to tell us that it was attempted murder?

(One red light. There is an immediate reaction. Everyone speaks simultaneously.)

BRYAN. It's incredible! Absolutely incredible. It's impossible, I tell you, impossible!

BRENDA. This is nonsense. Poor Jenny doesn't know what she's doing.

EMMELINE. It's not true. She doesn't know what she's saying.

ROSS. Murder! Murder! It can't be murder! D'you mean someone got in?

(**GINSBERG** *silences them.*)

GINSBERG. Please. Quiet, please!

EMMELINE. She doesn't know what she's saying.

INSPECTOR. I think she does.

GINSBERG. Mrs. Wingfield, did some unknown person come in from outside and attack you?

(Two red lights sharply.)

Was it someone in the house who pushed you?

(There is a pause, then one red light.)

WINGFIELD. My God!

(The red light flashes several times.)

NURSE. Doctor, her pulse is quickening.

(*The* **INSPECTOR** *crosses to* **GINSBERG.**)

INSPECTOR. *(Confidentially.)* Not much further. We must have the name.

GINSBERG. Mrs. Wingfield, do you know who pushed you?

(One red light.)

I'm going to spell out the name. Do you understand?

(One red light.)

Good. A, B.

(One red light.)

B. Is that right?

(Several red lights.)

NURSE. Doctor! She's collapsed.

GINSBERG. It's no good. I daren't go on. Nurse!

(*The* **NURSE** *goes to the trolley and collects a hypodermic. She hands the syringe to* **GINSBERG.**)

Thank you.

(*He breaks the ampule head, fills the syringe and injects it in the* **PATIENT***'s arm.*)

Lansen.

*(**LANSEN** switches off the electrical apparatus and removes the bulb from the **PATIENT**'s hand. He wheels the electrical apparatus into the curtained recess then exits.)*

GINSBERG. Nurse, would you unplug the steriliser?

NURSE. Yes, Doctor.

*(The **NURSE** returns the syringe to the trolley and unplugs the steriliser.)*

WINGFIELD. Is she all right?

GINSBERG. The strain and excitement have been too much for her. She'll be all right. She must rest for a while. We should be able to resume in about half an hour.

WINGFIELD. I forbid you to go on with it. It's dangerous.

GINSBERG. I think you must allow me to be the best judge of that. We'll move Mrs. Wingfield up nearer the window. She'll be all right there.

*(The **NURSE** helps **GINSBERG** and they move the **PATIENT** over to the window.)*

EMMELINE. There's not much doubt is there, who she meant? "B."

*(She turns to **WINGFIELD**.)*

Not much doubt about that is there, Bryan?

WINGFIELD. You always hated me, Emmeline. You always had it in for me. I tell you here and now, I didn't try to kill my wife.

EMMELINE. Do you deny that you were having an affair with that woman there?

*(She points to **BRENDA**.)*

BRENDA. It's not true.

EMMELINE. Don't tell me that. You were head over ears in love with him.

BRENDA. All right, then. I *was* in love with him. But that was all over ages ago. He didn't really care for me. It's all over, I tell you. All over!

EMMELINE. In that case it seems odd you stayed on as his secretary.

BRENDA. I didn't want to go. I – oh, all right, then! *(Passionately.)* I still wanted to be near him.

EMMELINE. And perhaps you thought that if Jenny were out of the way, you'd console him very nicely and be Mrs. Wingfield Number Two.

WINGFIELD. Emmeline, for heaven's sake!

EMMELINE. Perhaps it's "B" for Brenda.

BRENDA. You horrible woman! I hate you. It's not true.

ROSS. Bryan and Brenda. It seems to narrow it down to one of you two all right.

WINGFIELD. I wouldn't say that. It could be "B" for brother, couldn't it? Or Bill?

ROSS. She always called me William.

WINGFIELD. After all, who stands to gain by poor Jenny's death? Not me. It's you. You and Emmeline. It's you two who get her money.

GINSBERG. Please – please! I can't have all this argument. Nurse, will you take them down to the waiting room.

NURSE. Yes, Doctor.

ROSS. We can't stay cooped up in a little room with all of us slanging each other.

INSPECTOR. You can go where you please on the hospital premises, but none of you is actually to leave the place. *(Sharply.)* Is that understood?

BRYAN. All right.

ROSS. Yes.

EMMELINE. I have no wish to leave. My conscience is clear.

(**BRENDA** *approaches* **EMMELINE**.)

BRENDA. I think you did it.

EMMELINE. *(Sharply.)* What do you mean?

BRENDA. You hate her, you've always hated her. And you get the money, you and your brother.

EMMELINE. My name does not begin with a "B," I'm thankful to say.

BRENDA. *(Excitedly.)* No but it needn't.

(She turns to the **INSPECTOR**.*)*

Supposing that, after all, Mrs. Wingfield didn't see who it was who pushed her off the balcony.

EMMELINE. She has told us that she did.

BRENDA. But supposing that she didn't. Don't you see what a temptation it might be to her? She was jealous of me and Bryan, oh yes, she knew about us and she was jealous. And when that machine there gave her a chance to get back at us, at me – don't you see how tempting it was to say, "Brenda pushed me." It could have been like that, it could!

INSPECTOR. A little far-fetched.

BRENDA. No, it isn't! Not to a jealous woman. You don't know what women are like when they're jealous. And she'd been cooped up there in her room, thinking, suspecting, wondering if Bryan and I were still carrying on together. It isn't far-fetched, I tell you. It could easily be true.

(She looks at **WINGFIELD**.*)*

WINGFIELD. *(Thoughtfully.)* It is quite possible, you know, Inspector.

*(***BRENDA** *turns back to* **EMMELINE**.*)*

BRENDA. And you *do* hate her.

EMMELINE. Me? My own sister?

BRENDA. I've seen you looking at her often. You were in love with Bryan, he was half engaged to you and then Jenny came home from abroad and cut you out. Oh, she told me the whole story one day. You've never forgiven her. I think you've hated her ever since. I think that you came into her room that day and you saw her leaning over the balcony and it was too good a chance to be missed. You came up behind her and pushed her over!

EMMELINE. Inspector! Can't you stop this kind of thing?

INSPECTOR. I don't know that I want to, Miss Ross. I find it all very informative.

GINSBERG. I'm afraid I must insist on your leaving now. The patient must rest. We should be able to resume in twenty minutes. Nurse will take you downstairs.

NURSE. Yes, Doctor.

(She holds open the door. **ROSS, EMMELINE, WINGFIELD,** *and* **BRENDA** *move to exit.)*

INSPECTOR. Miss Ross, would you mind waiting a moment?

(They all pause briefly then **BRENDA** *exits followed by* **ROSS,** *the* **NURSE,** *and* **WINGFIELD.**)

EMMELINE. Well, what is it?

(The **INSPECTOR** *indicates a chair.* **EMMELINE** *sits.* **GINSBERG** *watches attentively.)*

INSPECTOR. There are one or two questions I should like to put to you. I didn't want to embarrass your brother.

EMMELINE. *(Sharply.)* Embarrass William? You don't know him. He has no self-respect at all. Never ashamed to admit that he doesn't know where to turn for the next penny!

INSPECTOR. *(Politely.)* That's very interesting but it was your brother-in-law that I thought might be embarrassed by the questions I am about to ask you.

EMMELINE. *(Surprised.)* Oh, Bryan. What do you want to know?

INSPECTOR. Miss Ross, you know the family very well. A person of your – intelligence would not be deceived as to what went on in it. You know the lives of your sister and your brother-in-law and what the relations were between them. It is reasonable that, up to now, you would say as little as you could. But now that you know what our suspicions are and the way they have been confirmed only a minute or two ago – well, that alters matters, doesn't it?

EMMELINE. Yes, I suppose it does. What do you want me to tell you?

INSPECTOR. This affair between Mr. Wingfield and Miss Jackson, was it serious?

EMMELINE. Not on his part. His affairs never are.

INSPECTOR. There actually *was* an affair?

EMMELINE. Of course. You heard her. She as good as admitted it.

INSPECTOR. You know it of your own knowledge?

EMMELINE. I could tell you various details to prove it but I do not propose to do so. You will have to accept my word for it.

INSPECTOR. It started when?

EMMELINE. Nearly a year ago.

INSPECTOR. And Mrs. Wingfield found out about it?

EMMELINE. Yes.

INSPECTOR. And what was her attitude?

EMMELINE. She taxed Bryan with it.

INSPECTOR. And he?

EMMELINE. He denied it, of course. Told her she was imagining things. You know what men are! Lie their way out of anything!

(The **INSPECTOR** *and* **GINSBERG** *exchange a look.)*

She wanted him to send the girl away, but he wouldn't – said she was far too good a secretary to lose.

INSPECTOR. But Mrs. Wingfield was very unhappy about it?

EMMELINE. Very.

INSPECTOR. Unhappy enough to want to take her own life?

EMMELINE. Not if she'd been well and strong. But her illness got her down. And she got all kinds of fancies.

GINSBERG. *(Curiously.)* What kinds of fancies, Miss Ross?

EMMELINE. Just fancies.

INSPECTOR. Why was Mrs. Wingfield left alone that afternoon?

EMMELINE. She preferred it. One of us always offered to sit with her but she had her books and her radio. For some reason she preferred to be alone.

INSPECTOR. Whose idea was it to send the nurse off duty?

GINSBERG. In private nursing that's standard practice. She would have two hours off every afternoon.

INSPECTOR. Miss Jackson has told us that, "It was all over ages ago," referring to her affair with Mr. Wingfield. Do you say that was not so?

EMMELINE. I think they broke with each other for a while. Or possibly they were very careful. But at the time of the accident it was on again all right. Oh yes!

INSPECTOR. You seem very sure of that.

EMMELINE. I lived in the house, didn't I?

(She pauses.)

And I'll show you something.

(She takes a piece of paper out of her handbag and hands it to the **INSPECTOR.***)*

I found it in the big Ming vase on the hall table. They used it as a post box it seems.

INSPECTOR. *(Reading.)* "Darling, we must be careful. I think she suspects. B."

(He looks at **GINSBERG.***)*

EMMELINE. It's Bryan's writing all right. So, you see!

GINSBERG. Do you mind if I ask a question or two?

INSPECTOR. No Doctor, please do.

GINSBERG. I'm interested in those "fancies" you mentioned, Miss Ross. You had some particular fancy in mind, I think.

EMMELINE. Just a sick woman's imaginings. She was ill, you see and she felt she wasn't making the progress she should have done.

GINSBERG. And she thought there was a reason for that?

EMMELINE. She was – just upset.

*(**INSPECTOR** leans forward, stressing his words.)*

INSPECTOR. *She thought there was a reason for it.*

EMMELINE. *(Uneasily.)* Well – yes.

GINSBERG. *(Quietly.)* She thought those two were poisoning her? That's it, isn't it?

(There is a pause.)

EMMELINE. *(Reluctantly.)* Yes.

GINSBERG. She said so to you?

EMMELINE. Yes.

GINSBERG. And what did you say?

EMMELINE. I told her it was all nonsense of course.

GINSBERG. Did you take any steps yourself?

EMMELINE. I don't know what you mean.

GINSBERG. Did you discuss it with the doctor attending her? Take any samples of food?

EMMELINE. *(Shocked.)* Of course not. It was just a sick woman's fancy.

GINSBERG. Well it happens, you know. Far more often than is known. The symptoms of arsenic poisoning, it's almost always arsenic, are practically indistinguishable from gastric disorders.

EMMELINE. Bryan couldn't – he just couldn't.

GINSBERG. It might have been the girl.

EMMELINE. Yes. Yes, I suppose so. *(Sighing.)* Well, we shall never know now.

GINSBERG. You're quite wrong there, Miss Ross. There are ways of telling. Traces of arsenic can be found in the hair, you know and in the finger nails.

EMMELINE. *(Rising.)* I can't believe it! I can't believe it of Bryan!

*(She turns to the **INSPECTOR** agitatedly.)*

Do you want me any longer, Inspector?

INSPECTOR. No, Miss Ross.

*(**EMMELINE** holds out her hand for the paper she gave to the **INSPECTOR**.)*

INSPECTOR. I'll keep this. It's evidence.

EMMELINE. Yes, of course.

*(**EMMELINE** exits.)*

GINSBERG. Well, we got something.

INSPECTOR. Yes.

(He sits in the elbow chair and looks at the piece of paper.)

From the Ming vase in the hall. Interesting.

GINSBERG. It's his writing?

INSPECTOR. Oh yes, it's Bryan Wingfield's writing all right. You know, he was quite a one for the ladies. Bowled them over like ninepins. Unfortunately they always took him seriously.

GINSBERG. Doesn't strike me as the Casanova type. Writes all those historical novels. Very erudite.

INSPECTOR. There's quite a lot of dirt in history.

GINSBERG. So it wasn't all over!

INSPECTOR. Get four people all het up and accusing each other, get an embittered and malicious woman on her own and invite her to spill the beans. It gives one some material to work on, doesn't it?

GINSBERG. In addition to what you had already. What did you have?

INSPECTOR. *(Smiling.)* Just some good solid facts. I went into the financial angle. Bryan Wingfield's a poor man, his wife's a rich woman. Her life's insured in favour of him, not for a very large sum, but it would enable him to marry again if he wanted to. Her money came to her in trust. If she dies childless, it's divided between her brother and sister. The brother's a wastrel, always trying to get money out of his rich sister. According to Bryan, she told her brother she wasn't going to pay for him any more. *(Thoughtfully.)* But I dare say she would have done – in the end.

GINSBERG. So which is it? B for Bryan? B for Brenda? B for Brother Bill? Or Emmeline without a B?

INSPECTOR. Emmeline without the – Emmeline? Wait a minute – something I heard this afternoon while they were all here.

(He pauses.)

No, it's gone.

GINSBERG. Could it be B for burglar?

INSPECTOR. No, that's definitely out. We've got conclusive evidence on that point. The road was up in front of the house and there was a constable on duty there. Both the side and the front gate were directly under his eye. Nobody entered or left the house, that afternoon.

GINSBERG. You know, you asked me to co-operate but you were very careful not to put all your cards on the table. Come on! What do you think?

INSPECTOR. It's not a question of thinking. I know.

GINSBERG. What?

INSPECTOR. I may be wrong, but I don't think so. You think it over.

*(**GINSBERG** enumerates on his fingers.)*

You've got seven minutes.

GINSBERG Huh? Oh, yes.

*(He rises and moves to the **PATIENT**. The **INSPECTOR** follows.)*

Mrs. Wingfield. Thank you for your help, Mrs. Wingfield. We come now to the crucial moment in the experiment.

INSPECTOR. Mrs. Wingfield, we are about to leave you here, apparently unguarded. None of the suspects know that you regained your powers of speech yesterday. They don't know that you did not in fact see who pushed you off that balcony. You realise what that means?

PATIENT. One of them will – will try to –

INSPECTOR. Someone will almost certainly enter this room.

GINSBERG. Are you sure you want to go through with this, Mrs. Wingfield?

PATIENT. Yes, yes. I must know – I must know who –

INSPECTOR. Don't be afraid. We shall be close at hand. If anyone approaches you or touches you –

PATIENT. I know what to do.

INSPECTOR. Thank you, Mrs. Wingfield, you're a wonderful woman. Just be brave for a few moments longer and we shall trap our killer. Trust me. Trust both of us, eh?

GINSBERG. Ready?

INSPECTOR. Right.

*(**GINSBERG** crosses to the doors and holds one open.)*

GINSBERG. Why don't you come into my office? In view of this poisoning suggestion you might like to look over the files.

INSPECTOR. Yes, I'd like another look at those x-ray plates too, if I may.

*(He switches off the lights and they exit. There is a pause. In the darkness a figure is seen entering holding a small syringe and making straight for the **PATIENT**.)*

PATIENT. Help! Help!

*(The figure quickly slips behind the recess curtain. The **INSPECTOR** enters.)*

INSPECTOR. All right, Mrs. Wingfield, we're here!

*(**GINSBERG** follows. He switches on the lights.)*

PATIENT. Help! Murder!

(She points to the curtain.)

There!

*(The **INSPECTOR** looks to **GINSBERG**.)*

INSPECTOR. Is she all right?

GINSBERG. She's all right. You've been very brave, Mrs. Wingfield.

INSPECTOR. Thank you, Mrs. Wingfield. The killer has played right into our hands. That note in the Ming vase was all I needed. Bryan Wingfield would hardly need to write secret notes to a secretary he sees every day. He wrote that note to someone else. And that constable on duty. He swears that nobody entered or left the house that afternoon.

(He moves slowly to the curtain.)

So it seems you didn't take your off duty walk that day. You may come out from behind that curtain now, Nurse Bond.

*(***NURSE BOND*** emerges. Blackout.)*

End of Play

The Wasp's Nest

CHARACTERS

CHARLES HARBOROUGH
CLAUD LANGDON
NINA BELLAMY
HERCULE POIROT

SETTING

The garden of Charles Harborough's house about half an hour before sunset on a summer's evening.

THE WASP'S NEST was originally a television play broadcast on the BBC on 18 June 1937. It was broadcast live from Alexandra Palace as part of the programme Theatre Parade. It was directed by George More O'Ferrall and the cast was as follows:

CHARLES HARBOROUGH .... D.A. Clarke-Smith
CLAUD LANGDON .... Wallace Douglas
NINA BELLAMY .... Antoinette Cellier
HERCULE POIROT .... Francis L. Sullivan

(The garden of **CHARLES HARBOROUGH***'s house. There is a wall with a door leading to the road. Near the door is a tall shrub. There is a table with drinks and garden chairs and an old tree root can be seen which contains a wasp's nest.* **NINA BELLAMY** *and* **CLAUD LANGDON** *are together. She is a pretty girl of twenty. At the moment she looks worried and upset. He is a good looking fellow of twenty-seven. He has a sullen expression on his face and is refusing to look at her.)*

NINA. *(Pleadingly.)* You do see how it was, don't you, Claud?

CLAUD. *(Reluctantly.)* Yes, I see.

NINA. And you forgive me?

(He does not answer.)

You do forgive me?

CLAUD. *(Impatiently.)* Oh, of course, of course! We've been over all that.

(He speaks to himself.)

But it's a bad show.

NINA. What?

CLAUD. Nothing, my dear.

NINA. You're so queer and unlike yourself.

CLAUD. Well, I feel rather badly about the business that's all.

NINA. It was my fault – all my fault. I blame myself bitterly.

CLAUD. You mustn't do that. It was my fault as much as yours. I was a bad tempered overbearing brute. No wonder you couldn't put up with me.

*(**HERCULE POIROT** enters. He stands in the doorway unnoticed, observing the two young people.)*

NINA. Yes, but I needn't have –

CLAUD. *(Impatiently.)* Oh, don't let's go over it all again.

NINA. I want you to understand.

CLAUD. I do understand.

NINA. And you do forgive me?

*(**CLAUD** takes **NINA** in his arms and kisses her gently.)*

And now you really have forgiven me?

CLAUD. For the thousandth time, yes!

NINA. *(Recoiling.)* But you are still angry, though.

CLAUD. Let's wash the subject out once and for all. Are you coming?

NINA. Not now. I'm waiting to see Charles.

CLAUD. *(Rudely.)* And more talk – talk – talk! Sorry, Nina, I'm in a bad mood today.

*(He turns sharply to exit and collides with **POIROT**.)*

POIROT. Pardon!

CLAUD. Sorry. My fault.

POIROT. Not at all, Mr. Langdon.

CLAUD. *(Surprised.)* You know me?

POIROT. I saw your name, *(Pause.)* at the chemist's shop.

*(**CLAUD** looks a little disconcerted.)*

CLAUD. Oh! The chemist's shop...

POIROT. Precisely. The chemist's shop.

CLAUD. *(Uncertainly.)* Oh!

*(He exits brusquely. **POIROT** bows politely to **NINA**.)*

POIROT. Mademoiselle!

(He looks slowly round as though in search of something.)

NINA. *(Coldly.)* Do you – er – want anything?

POIROT. It is true that I search for something.

NINA. What?

POIROT. A wasp's nest.

(**NINA** *looks at him as if he is mad.)*

NINA. These are private grounds, you know.

POIROT. *(Searching.)* Mais oui, mais oui.

NINA. So unless you wish to see Mr. Harborough –

POIROT. *(Absently.)* Monsieur Harborough, yes.

NINA. *(Sharply.)* This is Mr. Harborough's estate.

POIROT. I know. It is to see my friend Monsieur Harborough that I come.

NINA. *(Relieved.)* Oh, I see!

POIROT. *(Cheekily.)* So you see, Mademoiselle, I am not quite so mad as you think.

NINA. Oh, I didn't –

POIROT. But you did. You showed it most plainly. Now however, you are reassured. I am the friend of the family. My character is cleared.

NINA. I did think that perhaps –

(She breaks off and laughs.)

I suppose I showed it rather plainly.

POIROT. I am very quick to see things.

(He looks at her attentively.)

I can see something else. That you are worried, Mademoiselle.

NINA. Oh!

(She turns abruptly away. **CHARLES HARBOROUGH**, *a man of about forty, enters.)*

CHARLES. *(Surprised.)* Nina!

NINA. *(Nervously.)* Yes, I – I wanted to see you.

(**CHARLES** *catches sight of* **POIROT**.)

CHARLES. By all that's wonderful, Hercule Poirot!

(He shakes him warmly by the hand.)

NINA. *(Startled.)* Hercule Poirot!

CHARLES. Monsieur Poirot – Miss Bellamy. The prince of detectives, Nina. The terror of evil-doers.

(He turns back to **POIROT**.)

And what brings you to this quiet part of the world?

POIROT. You remember saying to me if ever I am in this part of the country to look you up. That is right, is it not? Look you up!

CHARLES. Quite right.

POIROT. Eh bien, I take you at your word.

CHARLES. Splendid. Have a drink.

NINA. I – I think I'll be going Charles. I'll see you tomorrow.

(She slips out quickly.)

POIROT. No whisky – a little plain soda only. That was your fiancée, was it not? All the congratulations.

CHARLES. Oh – er – you saw?

POIROT. But yes, I read the announcement three days ago. A marriage arranged between Charles Harborough and Nina, the daughter of Colonel Bellamy.

(He raises his glass.)

À votre santé.

(**CHARLES** *turns away sharply with a gesture that might be embarrassment or dislike.)*

You are a fortunate man.

CHARLES. *(Gruffly.)* Yes.

(They sit.)

POIROT. The young lady is charming – quite charming.

(There is a pause.)

Pardon me if I commit an indiscretion – the lady was engaged before she met you?

CHARLES. Yes.

POIROT. To a Mr. Langdon?

CHARLES. Yes.

POIROT. So she has done the jilt, as you say. She has turned him downwards for you?

CHARLES. Yes, but –

POIROT. Which is all very well for you, but not so agreeable for him, eh?

CHARLES. *(Stiffly.)* It's a lady's privilege to change her mind, and if you'll excuse my saying so, Monsieur Poirot, jilting is rather an offensive expression.

POIROT. *(Quickly.)* Ah! Pardon.

CHARLES. *(Sententiously.)* It's better to find out a mistake in time.

POIROT. Much better. And Mr. Langdon, what does he think?

CHARLES. Langdon's taken it very well, taken it like a man, in fact.

POIROT. Like a man. How does a man take a thing of that kind?

CHARLES. Like a sportsman.

POIROT. *(Thoughtfully.)* Ah!

CHARLES. You've not told me what you are doing down in this part of the world. On holiday, I suppose?

POIROT. *(Slowly.)* No, I am not on holiday. I am here on business.

CHARLES. Business?

(He stares curiously at **POIROT.***)*

You mean you are here professionally – as a detective?

POIROT. Yes.

CHARLES. *(Curiously.)* I suppose I mustn't ask you anything about your investigations?

POIROT. On the contrary, I should prefer that you asked.

CHARLES. You are investigating a – burglary?

POIROT. Something far more serious.

CHARLES. What?

POIROT. *(Quietly.)* Murder.

CHARLES. *(Startled.)* You mean –

POIROT. *(Impressively.)* Murder!

CHARLES. But I haven't heard of any murder.

POIROT. No, you would not have heard of it.

CHARLES. Who has been murdered?

POIROT. As yet, nobody.

CHARLES. Oh!

(He leans back with a laugh. **POIROT** *remains serious.)*

POIROT. That is why I said you would not have heard of it. Nobody has been murdered yet. I am investigating a crime that has not yet taken place.

CHARLES. But look here, that's nonsense!

POIROT. Not at all. If one can investigate a crime before it has happened, surely that is very much better than investigating it afterwards. You see, one might prevent it.

CHARLES. You're not serious, Monsieur Poirot?

POIROT. But yes, I am serious.

*(**CHARLES** is impressed in spite of himself.)*

CHARLES. You really believe that a murder is going to be committed?

POIROT. I know it.

CHARLES. You are making me feel quite eerie.

(He shivers.)

Someone must be walking over my grave.

(There is a short pause then **POIROT** *leans forward with a change of manner.)*

POIROT. Tell me, Mr. Harborough, have you a wasp's nest in this garden?

(**CHARLES** *stares at him.*)

CHARLES. Rather odd your saying that.

POIROT. No, it is not odd, really.

CHARLES. *(Continuing.)* But as a matter of fact there is a nest over there.

(He nods towards the tree root.)

I'm expecting Langdon any minute to take it for me. He's rather good at that sort of thing. Just taken four in his own garden. My gardener's a fool at the job. I said so and Langdon insisted on coming over this evening and doing it.

POIROT. What method does he employ?

CHARLES. Squirts petrol down with a syringe.

POIROT. There is another method. Cyanide of potassium.

CHARLES. Yes, but that's dangerous stuff.

POIROT. Deadly poison.

CHARLES. It's not the kind of stuff I care to have about the place.

POIROT. And yet – just now, Mr. Langdon was buying cyanide of potassium at the chemist.

CHARLES. *(Shocked.)* What?

POIROT. That surprises you?

CHARLES. Yes, it does. What did he say he wanted it for?

POIROT. To take a wasp's nest in your garden, I understood.

CHARLES. Nonsense! He knows I won't have that stuff used. He agreed himself that petrol is much safer and just as efficacious.

POIROT. Then it was not you who asked him to get cyanide?

CHARLES. *(Emphatically.)* Certainly not.

(**POIROT** *relaxes and sits back.*)

POIROT. That is odd.

CHARLES. It's very odd, very odd indeed.

(He looks unhappily at **POIROT** *who returns his glance steadily. A feeling of tension grows.)*

CHARLES. You're not – not suggesting – no, that's impossible.

POIROT. What is impossible?

CHARLES. That Langdon is – oh! But that's fantastic.

POIROT. Is it?

(He gives **CHARLES** *a very significant glance.)*

CHARLES. So that's why you came down here, to warn me against Langdon.

(He springs up.)

Oh, but it's absurd.

POIROT. Listen. When I came here this evening, Miss Bellamy and Langdon were here in the garden. They did not observe me. She was talking to him, asking him to forgive her, begging him to tell her that he "understood."

CHARLES. How like a woman.

POIROT. Yes.

CHARLES. Well?

POIROT. So that is all you have to say! Well? And suppose it is not well.

CHARLES. I don't know what you're driving at.

POIROT. I will be more clear. Suppose that Mr. Langdon does not find it well at all. That he neither forgives nor understands, that he is planning revenge.

CHARLES. No, no, that's ridiculously melodramatic. Langdon's said to have the devil of a temper, but he would never. Why, he's carried on absolutely as usual. He's been amazingly decent over the whole business. In fact, he's gone out of his way to be extra friendly with me since – since it happened.

POIROT. Amazingly decent. You use the word amazingly – but you are not amazed. Now me, I find his behaviour very odd.

CHARLES. Yes, but you, excuse me, are a foreigner.

POIROT. I knew you would say that! Nobody who is not of the Latin races can feel jealousy – c'est entendu! But your police courts give that statement the lie. Come, I will put a case to you. Here is a young man badly hit because he has been turned downwards – you see how idiomatic I am! Eh bien, he sets the teeth, he stiffens the knees, he conceals the emotions and he determines to behave exactly as usual – even more so. He will show the world that he is not hard hit at all – au contraire! Life is very amusing! You are engaged today, you are jilted tomorrow, and what of it all?

CHARLES. That's exactly what I have been saying.

POIROT. But supposing that is all the pose – the gigantic bluff. *(Slowly.)* Jealousy...hate...revenge.

CHARLES. That sort of thing simply doesn't happen in England.

POIROT. The English are sometimes incredibly stupid. They think they can deceive anyone, but that no one can deceive them. The sportsman, the good fellow, never will they believe evil of him. And because they are brave but stupid, *(Significantly.)* sometimes they die.

(**CHARLES** *speaks without conviction.)*

CHARLES. I don't believe Langdon would hurt a fly.

POIROT. The lives of flies are not my concern, and though you say that Mr. Langdon is so tender of them, yet you forget that he is even now preparing to take the life of several hundred wasps!

(**CHARLES** *stands irresolute, looking at him.* **POIROT** *springs up and approaches him. He takes* **CHARLES** *by the shoulders and shakes him.)*

Rouse yourself, my friend, rouse yourself! And look where I am pointing.

(He points towards the tree root.)

There, on the bank, by that old root. See you the wasps returning home, placid at the end of the day? In a little hour comes destruction and they know it not. There is no one to tell them. They have not, it seems, a Hercule

Poirot. I told you, Mr. Harborough, that I came here on business. Murder is my business. It is my business before it has happened as well as afterwards. I am here to prevent this murder – and I shall prevent it!

(There is a pause. **POIROT** *calms himself.)*

What time is Langdon coming to do this business of the wasp's nest?

*(***CHARLES** *is convinced but automatically protests.)*

CHARLES. Langdon would never –

POIROT. At what time?

CHARLES. At ten o'clock.

*(***POIROT** *consults his watch.)*

POIROT. And it is now half past nine, good.

CHARLES. But I tell you Langdon would never –

POIROT. Ah, mon dieu! Langdon would never, Langdon would never! Have it your own way. Langdon would never! C'est entendu!

(He readies himself to leave.)

All the same, I return here at ten o'clock.

CHARLES. But really –

POIROT. Langdon would never! C'est entendu. I return only to amuse myself by seeing one of your English sports – the taking of the wasp's nest. I do not stay to argue with you now, because I should only enrage myself. Au revoir till ten o'clock.

(He bows and makes to exit. **CHARLES** *shrugs his shoulders and turns away. He picks up a glass from the table.* **POIROT** *opens the door but as he is about to go, he draws quickly back, shutting the door behind him and hiding behind the shrub.* **CLAUD** *enters carrying a small glass syringe.)*

CHARLES. *(Turning.)* Hullo, you're late.

CLAUD. Just on time, I think. But it's still rather light. We'd better give the last stragglers time to return home. You've got the stuff all right?

CHARLES. Yes, I've got the stuff. Have a drink?

CLAUD. Thanks.

(**CHARLES** *pours a whisky and soda and gives it to him. He then pours one for himself.* **CLAUD** *lays down the syringe on the table.)*

(Sitting.) Nina tells me that the famous Monsieur Poirot is down here.

CHARLES. Yes. He came to look me up.

CLAUD. What's he doing down here?

CHARLES. Possibly his job.

CLAUD. You mean detecting?

CHARLES. Possibly.

CLAUD. But, I say, there isn't anything to detect, is there?

(There is a pause.)

Is there?

CHARLES. Perhaps Monsieur Poirot knows better. *(Grimly.)* Perhaps, by this time tomorrow there may be something to detect.

CLAUD. So there may. Well, cheerio.

(He raises his glass.)

CHARLES. Cheerio.

(**CLAUD** *drinks then sets down his empty glass.* **CHARLES** *only puts his glass to his lips. There is a pause.)*

I wonder, Langdon, if you'd mind coming back tomorrow and taking the nest then – well, tonight I'd rather give it a miss.

CLAUD. Certainly if you like.

(He becomes suddenly incoherent.)

I'm sorry if – did Nina – or –

CHARLES. *(Harshly.)* Let's leave all that.

CLAUD. Right. Tomorrow then.

CHARLES. Yes, tomorrow. Goodbye, Langdon.

CLAUD. Goodnight.

CHARLES. Goodbye.

(**CLAUD** *exits. Left alone,* **CHARLES'** *expression slowly changes. He laughs silently. His face becomes the face of the devil. He looks not quite sane. After his mirth is over he takes a small wide-mouthed bottle from his pocket. It has a few crystals in it, which he shakes into his whisky and soda.)*

(Then with a handkerchief he carefully wipes fingerprints from the bottle and throws it into the garden. **POIROT** *emerges from behind the shrub, coming up noiselessly behind him.* **CHARLES** *picks up his glass and puts it to his lips. Before he drinks,* **POIROT** *deftly seizes it from him.)*

(Turning.) What –

(**POIROT** *steps out of* **CHARLES'** *reach.)*

POIROT. I think I had better drink this.

(He raises the glass to his lips. **CHARLES** *screams in frenzy.)*

CHARLES. Don't drink it! For God's sake don't drink it! It's poisoned, I tell you, poisoned!

(**POIROT** *with a smile drinks.* **CHARLES** *stands appalled shaking all over.* **POIROT** *makes a grimace, wipes his lips with his handkerchief and replaces the glass on the table.)*

My God, cyanide of potassium.

POIROT. No, my friend, you are in error. You see, just now, I made a little exchange.

(He takes a bottle from his pocket.)

This is the cyanide you asked Claud Langdon to get for you. In your pocket I placed a similar bottle containing washing soda. It was quite simple – a clever pickpocket taught me the trick. I excited myself, I take you by the shoulders – so – and sapristi, the change is made.

CHARLES. *(Broken.)* How did you know?

POIROT. I guessed, my friend. I guessed right, that is all.

CHARLES. But how did you guess?

POIROT. I must begin that story yesterday when I saw you come out of a certain doctor's door in Harley Street. I know that doctor, I know for what one consults him, and I saw your face. It was the face of a doomed man.

CHARLES. Doomed – doomed – he gave me two months to live.

POIROT. I was close by you, but you did not see me. You were too preoccupied. And suddenly I saw your expression change. I saw in your eyes that of which I spoke to you this evening – hate – jealousy – the desire for revenge. You did not trouble to conceal them, you thought there was no need. And then you grinned – a devilish exultant grin it was, and I knew something. I knew that I was looking at a murderer. Do not ask me how I knew, just let me assure you that Hercule Poirot could not be mistaken on that point. I was looking at a murderer, but as yet a murderer only in intention. As I tell you, murder is my business. I came down here today to look into the matter.

CHARLES. Go on.

POIROT. I have seen the announcement of your engagement in the paper. The first thing I hear down here is the story of Miss Bellamy's prior attachment to Claud Langdon. Then I happen to go into the chemist and this same Langdon is there buying cyanide of potassium. So it looks, does it not, as though my ideas were all wrong – as though if murder were being planned, it is Claud Langdon who should be planning to murder you. He has the motive and he has the means. So I come up here to see what is the truth of the wasp's nest story, and I see the two young people and I realise without a doubt that it is Langdon whom she loves.

She has quarrelled with him and got engaged to you in a fit of pique, but now she is asking him to forgive and take her back and trying to make him understand how it all came about. So, after all, it is you who have a motive for murder. It is he who has taken the girl from you. And then I lay a few little traps. I speak of the cyanide, and you deny having asked him to get it for you, but I see your eyelids flicker and I know that you are lying. I pretend to have suspicions and very cleverly you increase them. I am to be your star witness against Langdon.

CHARLES. Do you suggest that I meant to poison Langdon with cyanide?

POIROT. No, your crime was cleverer than that! The cyanide was for yourself – a quick death instead of the lingering one the specialist had foretold for you. Langdon was to be accused of your murder. Miss Bellamy's engagement to you would give the motive. Then there would be the purchase of the poison. He would say that he had done that at your request, but then I should give evidence that that was not so, that you had expressly denied having done any such thing. So motive, means and finally – opportunity. He comes up and has a drink with you this evening – and you are found dead with the remains of cyanide in your glass. And so Claud Langdon would have been hanged and Miss Bellamy's heart would have been broken.

*(**CHARLES**' voice is thick with passion.)*

CHARLES. And why not? Why not? Why should he have everything and I nothing? Why should he live and I die? Why should he have Nina? Nina! Nina, who made a fool of me. I hated them both. I wanted them to suffer – suffer – as I suffer! *(Angrily.)* And you – you –

POIROT. I have saved you. Oh, not from death. Death comes to all of us sooner or later. But I have saved you from sending an innocent man to his death, and from ruining a girl's life. Even now in your heart, you are glad that I came here today. *(Compellingly.)* Tell me, my friend, are you not glad that you will die an honest man and not a murderer, thanks to Hercule Poirot.

CHARLES. I – I –

(He breaks down. **NINA** *and* **CLAUD** *enter. It has grown almost dark.)*

NINA. Is that you, Charles? We came – I felt we must come tonight –

CLAUD. *(Interrupting.)* Look here, Harborough, the truth of the matter is –

CHARLES. *(Brusquely.)* I know the truth. Nina cares for you, Langdon, and always has. Well, that's all right. No bones broken. Do you mind if I leave you with Monsieur Poirot? He's rather pleased with himself just now. And perhaps he's right.

(He puts a hand on **NINA***'s shoulder.)*

Bless you, my dear, be happy.

(He exits. **NINA** *turns to* **POIROT***.)*

NINA. Why are you pleased with yourself?

POIROT. I have succeeded in the business that brought me down here.

NINA. *(Doubtfully.)* Oh?

POIROT. *(Happily.)* And now, a little relaxation. For a change I experience the reactions of murder – murder on a grand scale, you comprehend.

(He fills the cyanide bottle with water, shakes it, then tip-toes to the wasp's nest with exaggerated caution. Averting his head, he pours it down a hole in the root. He contemplates the results.)

POIROT. Voilà. They die the death. Alas, poor wasps, there is none to save you.

(He turns to the others.)

You see, they had no Hercule Poirot!

End of Play

THE AGATHA CHRISTIE COLLECTION

Agatha Christie is regarded as the most successful female playwright of all time. Her illustrious dramatic career spans forty-two years, countless acclaimed original plays, several renowned novels adapted for stage, and numerous collections of thrilling one-act plays. Testament to Christie's longevity, these plays continue to engage great artists and enthral audiences today.

Since the première of her first play in 1930 the world of theatre has changed immeasurably, and so has the way plays are published and performed. Embarking upon a two-year project, Agatha Christie Limited sought to re-open Christie's distinguished body of dramatic work, looking to both original manuscripts and the most recent publications to create a "remastered" edition of each play. Each new text would contain only the words of Agatha Christie (or adaptors she personally worked with) and all extraneous materials that might come between the interpreter and the playwright would be removed, ultimately bringing the flavor and content of the texts closer to what the author would have delivered to the rehearsal room. Each new edition would then be specifically tailored to the needs and requirements of the professional twenty-first century artist.

The result is The Collection.

Whether in a classic revival or new approach, The Collection has been purposely assembled for the contemporary theatre professional. The choice and combination of plays offers something for all tastes and kinds of performance with the skill, imagination and genius of Agatha Christie's work now waiting to be explored anew in theatre.

For more information on The Collection, please visit
agathachristielimited.com/licensing/stage/browse-by-play

Lightning Source UK Ltd.
Milton Keynes UK
UKHW022050080120
356600UK00010B/649/P

9 780573 031045